COURAGE AND CALLING
The Study Guide

Courage and Calling
The Study Guide

Chapter-by-Chapter Questions and Exercises
for Reflection and Group Discussion

Soo-Inn Tan
&
Gordon T. Smith

Regent College Publishing
www.regentpublishing.com

Courage and Calling: The Study Guide
Copyright © 2008 Soo-Inn Tan and Gordon T. Smith

All rights reserved. No part of this publication may be reproduced, stored in a retrieval system, or transmitted, in any form or by any means, electronic, mechanical, photocopying, recording or otherwise, without the prior written permission of the author, except in the case of brief quotations embodied in critical articles and reviews.

Published 2008 by Regent College Publishing
5800 University Boulevard, Vancouver, BC V6T 2E4 Canada
Web: www.regentpublishing.com
E-mail: info@regentpublishing.com

Book design by Robert Hand
<roberthandcommunications.com>

Regent College Publishing is an imprint of the Regent Bookstore <www.regentbookstore.com>. Views expressed in works published by Regent College Publishing are those of the author and do not necessarily represent the official position of Regent College <www.regent-college.edu>.

ISBN-10: 1-57383-410-6
ISBN-13: 978-1-57383-410-0

Library and Archives Canada Cataloguing in Publication

Tan, Soo-Inn, 1955–
Courage and calling. The study guide / Soo-Inn Tan and Gordon T. Smith.

Study guide for Courage & Calling, by Gordon T. Smith.
Includes bibliographical references.
ISBN 978-1-57383-410-0

1. Vocation—Christianity—Study guides. I. Smith, Gordon T., 1953– .
Courage & calling. II. Title.

BV4740.S63 1999 Suppl.   248.4   C2008-900515-5

Contents

Part I
*Introduction: Making a Difference for Christ,
as Good Stewards of Our Lives / 9*

Part II
Courage and Calling: Chapter by Chapter

1. The Context of Our Lives and Work / 19
2. Seeking Congruence / 25
3. Chapters in Our Lives / 31
4. As Unto the Lord / 39
5. Thinking Vocationally / 45
6. Courage and Character / 51
7. The Capacity to Learn / 57
8. The Cross We Bear / 63
9. Working With and Within Organizations / 71
10. The Ordered Life / 79

Part III
Final Exercises and Conclusion / 87

Select Bibliography / 93

I

*Introduction: Making a Difference for Christ,
as Good Stewards of Our Lives*

Introduction

It has been about ten years since I—Gordon—wrote *Courage and Calling*. And it has often been mentioned that it would be good to have a workbook and study guide to assist readers as they think through and, perhaps with a small group, *talk* through the material in the book.

So, it has been a pleasure to team up with Soo-Inn Tan to pull together this study and group discussion guide. The first iterations of this book were used as part of the ministry of *NextUp*, a Malaysian-based ministry that seeks to help young adults discover their vocation so that they can pursue it faithfully. By teaming together, we are now able to make this resource available to a wider audience.

Courage and Calling raises the kinds of questions that require reflection and critical thought—about ourselves and our work. We have found that this personal reflection is enhanced if we can do it in community, with others with whom we are seeking together to be good stewards of our lives. This study guide seeks to foster this two-fold objective: to encourage good personal reflection and to encourage good conversation about our lives, our callings and the challenges of life and work in our generation.

The ideal is for these to come together. So the study guide encourages the reader to spend time in solitude—alone and in private, to raise and respond to critical questions that need to be considered if one is to come to vocational maturity. But then this personal time is complemented by group processes.

As you read *Courage and Calling* and use this Study Guide, consider the value of keeping a journal. Through this process, write daily in your journal—sometimes a more extensive series of thoughts, and sometimes just a line or two. The journal will keep the process current and help you keep track of the progress of your thoughts.

Then, as you make personal entries, you can let the group process challenge or support your individual reflections. These also need to be recorded in your journals.

Each chapter of this study guide will therefore call for both personal reflection and group discussion. Consider the following as an order or sequence:

1. Read the appropriate chapter in *Courage and Calling* and in the study guide; and read the assigned Scripture text in the study guide;

2. Complete the suggested personal responses and exercises;

3. In a small group, share with others your impressions from your reading and identify what emerged in the personal responses;

4. Let the personal responses lead to group discussion about what has emerged for each person and what, together, the group is learning about the meaning of vocation;

5. In the small group, give time at the end for prayer and a time of silence. Following the group discussion, when you are alone again, make a journal

entry identifying what impressed you about your own life and work (as a result of the group discussion).

The primary reference for this workbook is, of course, *Courage and Calling*—a book that calls us to a theologically sound understanding of vocation. The study guide will suggest practices by which we can each pursue our vocation faithfully, as good stewards of our lives.

In *Courage and Calling*, we note:

> For each individual there is a specific call—a defining purpose or mission, a reason for being. Every individual is called of God to respond uniquely through service in the world. We can only understand this second meaning of call in light of the first (i.e., the call to follow Jesus): when we fulfill our specific vocation we are living out the full implications of what it means to follow Jesus.
>
> Therefore, while we all have a general call to love God and neighbor, each of us follows our Lord differently. He calls us all to follow him, and once we accept that call each of us is honored with a unique call that is an integral part of what it means to follow him (p. 9).

The chapters of *Courage and Calling* cover the following:

Chapter One. *The Context of Our Work and Lives: A Theological Response.* Questions for this section will address concerns about the fundamental crises we face in the new millennium. They will consider what it means to respond theologically to these with a biblical consideration of work, vocation and self and how in the face of these challenges we can make a difference.

Chapter Two. *Seeking Congruence: The Nature of Vocational Integrity.* Questions for this section will examine the challenge for Christians to come to terms with their vocation. They will address in particular Smith's guidelines to help believers know what their callings may be and how one can be true to one's calling. We will seek to see how we can follow the suggestion to live with the tension between our own ideals/aspirations and an accurate reading of our actual circumstances.

Chapter Three. *Chapters in Our Lives.* Questions for this segment will examine the key features of the three divisions and how they impact one's vocation: adolescence through early adulthood; early to mid-adulthood; and, mid-adulthood to the senior years. As we will see, when it comes to living faithfully, we need to address the matter of vocation at each stage of our lives.

Chapter Four. *As Unto the Lord: The Pursuit of Excellence, Truth, Diligence & Generosity.* In this chapter, we are challenged to pursue our vocation with "excellence, truth, diligence, and generosity." Questions for this segment will explore what the four virtues really mean and how one can apply them in one's vocation. There will also be a brief discussion of the importance of Sabbath and its implications for a balanced life.

Chapter Five. *Thinking Vocationally.* Questions for this segment will seek to consider what it means to think vocationally. In particular they will look at the many advantages of thinking vocationally, as well as the main obstacles that prevent one from thinking vocationally. We will also study the need for the capabilities of retrospection and being fully present, for one to be able to think vocationally.

Chapter Six. *Courage and Character.* A central theme of this book and of the study guide is that "it takes courage to make a difference." Questions for this segment will examine what it means to have courage, paying particular attention to the character traits that accompany true courage. We will especially look at the reminder that we need both the grace of God and the encouragement of others to live with true courage.

Chapter Seven. *The Capacity to Learn.* This chapter stresses the need for continuous learning if we are to live vocationally. To appreciate this it is helpful to consider the four main ways in which people learn; and the chapter includes suggestions as to how we should use all four for our development. Questions for this segment will also examine how it is that wisdom integrates true learning.

Chapter Eight. *The Cross We Bear.* With this chapter, we are reminded that any discussion of vocation cannot avoid the "difficulties, setbacks, and disappointments" of life. And we have guidelines as to how we can make sense of pain and respond positively to it. In the same context, we speak of emotional health—what it is and how we can nurture it.

Chapter Nine. *Working With and Within Organizations.* This chapter points out that to pursue our vocations to the fullest we will have to work with others in the context of organizations. So we have suggestions as to how one can be effective within organizations. The chapter also addresses the matter of job change—when it is right for a Christian to resign from an organization and move on.

Chapter Ten. *The Ordered Life.* The book concludes with a proposal for a basic structure for our lives; one that will help our vocational development. The primary features of this structure are community and solitude.

The study guide is also divided into ten sections—each section tied to the corresponding chapter. We will suggest study questions, a Scripture text for meditation, guidelines for group discussion, suggestions for "further reading" and some supplemental questions for those who want to pursue the topic even further.

Let's begin with the *Introduction*, as we get into this exercise (pp. 9-11).

1. We read: "A calling is always a demonstration of the love of God and the initiative of God; but more, it is through vocation that we come to an appreciation that God takes us seriously."

    a. What catches your attention in this statement? What strikes you about this?

    b. What are other ways that can help you realize that God takes you seriously?

2. Note the suggestion that we think of the call of God in three distinct ways:

    "First, there is the call to be Christian."

    "Second, for each individual, there is a specific call—a defining purpose or mission, a reason for being."

    "Third, there is the calling we face each day in response to the multiple demands on our lives—our immediate duties and responsibilities."

    a. Identify your own sense of the first—what it means to be called to be a Christian.

    b. For the "second," how has this already been a significant expression of the "first" for you?

3. In the Introduction, we read that the focus of this book is the second sense, our unique mission in the world, "... our engagement with the world in response to God."

   a. How is this question relevant to you at this stage of your life? Elaborate.

   b. What is an ideal outcome for you through this process? A greater understanding of your vocation? Clarity about a critical career choice you need to make? Perhaps something else that you hope will come from this?

II

Courage and Calling: Chapter by Chapter

1

The Context of Our Lives and Work: A Theological Response

Focus: The Realities of Work and a Biblical Response

Scripture for Meditation
Exodus 20:8–11; Proverbs 31:10–31

Study Questions

1. We are reminded that we live in a time of rapid change and that this is "having a profound effect on the way we live, the way we work and the way we think about our lives and work" (pp. 15–20).

This will involve loss but, as noted, what we urgently need "is the capacity to see change as opportunity." In particular, consider these four crises we face today.

- The crisis of employment: ". . . the lack of employment or waged work is increasingly part of the modern economy."
- The crisis of confidence: ". . . changing circumstances leave us all with a lack of confidence that we can do what we are called to do."

- The crisis of focus: ". . . the crisis of hectic, unfocused activity."
- The crisis of meaning: "We all become confused about work and the meaning of work, and consequently we are perplexed about the meaning of who we are."

Read through the description of the four types of crises. Reflect on your own life in the light of what you have read and note evidence of each in your own work situation.

2. We are called to a theological response to the crises of the day (pp. 20–29). In particular, we need to recover the theologies of:

- Work: humankind was "created to work, and their work was meaningful."
- Vocation: ". . . a call of God to serve Him in the world . . . the reality and principle that all vocations are potentially sacred."
- Self: ". . . a person is created by God and has worth and significance."

a. Which of these captures your attention—perhaps the "theology" that you feel most needs attention in the life of the church?

b. "The recovery of a biblical theology of vocation leads us to a renewed appreciation of the full extent of God's kingdom. All vocations are sacred because the kingdom is not merely spiritual."

Consider in your own experience what a broad appreciation of vocation would mean for your life and work.

c. Throughout this chapter we are reminded that as

Christians we need to re-affirm the need to help Christians understand the value of who they are and what they do.

"The Bible affirms the essential worth and significance of each person: we are all created in the image of God, we are chosen and elect of God, and thus we have incomparable worth and significance in God's eyes."

How do we avoid the twin dangers of either thinking our work is of no spiritual significance, or trying to find our self worth and significance in our work rather than in God?

3. The purpose of the book restated:

> What follows is a study for people who are prepared to think honestly about their lives—who are willing to acknowledge the gifts and abilities they have from God, willing to be honest with themselves, willing to make some tough choices, and willing to do all of this in partnership with others (pp. 28–31).

Note then a number of challenges if we are serious about working through the book. Are we:

- Prepared to think honestly about our lives?
- Willing to acknowledge the gifts and abilities we have from God?
- Willing to be honest with ourselves?
- Willing to make some tough choices?
- Willing to do the above in partnership with others?

a. In light of the above challenges, do you think you are ready to work through *Courage and Calling*?

b. What are some challenges you will face? What help will you need?

4. Consider also the futility of regrets: "Without regret we will look to the present and the future, conscious of the tremendous potential we have because of the grace of God" (pp. 29–32).

   a. Are there any major regrets in your life that could impede your capacity to embrace your future?

5. "We long to find and do work that is meaningful, that makes a difference and needs to be done" (pp. 31–32).

   a. To what degree does the above statement describe you?

   b. What price are you willing to pay to make that statement come true for you?

6. This chapter profiles two assumptions for all who plan to work through the book: "that all people are responsible for the choices they make, and that these choices are meaningful and significant" (p. 28).

   a. Do you feel that the choices you make are "meaningful and significant?" How do you feel their significance—for yourself and for others who are affected by your decisions?

   b. Are you someone who normally takes responsibility for his or her life or do you often see yourself as a victim of forces not under your control?

Are you prepared to take responsibility of your own life now if you have never done so seriously before?

Interacting with Scripture

Read 1 Chronicles 12:32.

1. What qualified the men of Issachar to "know what Israel ought to do?"

2. What are some of the features of the working world today according to this chapter in *Courage and Calling*?

3. How are your decisions concerning work and vocation based on your "understanding of the times?"

For Further Reading

Brennfleck, Kevin and Kay Marie Brennfleck. "In Search of a Calling." Chap. 1 in *Live Your Calling: A Practical Guide to Finding and Fulfilling Your Mission in Life.* San Francisco, CA: Jossey-Bass, 2005.

Supplementary Questions to Help in Journaling

1. Write down the things about your work that give you the most joy. (Homemaking is also work; so is study!)

2. Write down those things about your work that frustrate you the most.

3. Write down a number of ways your faith makes a difference in your work.

2

Seeking Congruence: The Nature of Vocational Integrity

Focus: Discovering Our Vocation by Understanding Ourselves

Scripture for Meditation
Romans 12:1–9

Study Questions

1. Note the following statement from *Courage and Calling*: "The most critical thing to which we can give our attention is to come to terms with our vocation. Each of us individually must come to peace about what it is that we are called to do. Nothing matters more than this" (pp. 33–35).

   a. How much attention has the notion of calling or vocation received in the communities you belong to? How is calling usually defined in those communities?

   b. What has been your own experience in trying to discern your calling to date?

2. "There are some people whose vocation will actually be fulfilled outside of their occupation; their occupation is but their means of livelihood. And there are others who fulfill their vocation without being gainfully employed. Some people may not even begin to discover their vocation until after they have retired from a career. Thus it is not something we can necessarily demand or expect but rather a sheer gift if we are able to fulfill our vocation through an occupation." "We must be both reasonable and idealistic" (pp. 35–37).

   a. How do you feel about this statement? Does it encourage you? Or free you?

   b. If you have some inkling about your vocation at this time, do you think it can be fulfilled in the context of an occupation or not?

3. Know Yourself

"God has granted grace to each of us; therefore, we can take an honest, critical and discerning look at ourselves." "To live in truth we must be true to who we are. But this is not possible unless we know who we are: how God has made us, how we are unique, how God has enabled us to serve him in the church and in the world" (pp. 37–43).

   a. Does your church community encourage this kind of critical self-reflection? If so, how is it expressed? And if not, how is this evident?

   b. *Courage and Calling* suggests that we need to reflect on four key questions as a way of knowing ourselves:

      i. What do you do well? What are some of your more obvious gifts and abilities? Spiritual gifts? Natural abilities? Acquired skills and knowledge?

ii. What are some of your deepest desires? "When you set aside (your) longings for security, wealth, comfort, fame and even acceptance, what do (you) long for?" List the ten things that have brought you the greatest joy. What have they told you about yourself?

iii. "Our vocational identity is aligned in some way with how we uniquely see the pain and brokenness of the world. We all see the brokenness of the world through the very particular lenses of our own eyes and heart." Of the many needs that are found in the world, which type of need particularly bugs you? What keeps you awake at night? Romans 12:6–8 lists seven primary roles or means of engagement with the world. Read through the list and see which role best describes you.

iv. Have you ever done the Myers-Briggs Type Indicator instrument? Some other type of personality test? If you have, what did the results tell you about yourself? And what might it mean as you come to terms with your own vocation? What are you freed not to be and do; and what are you drawn to?

c. *Courage and Calling* notes that when we have some idea of "our gifts and abilities, our deepest desires, how we see the brokenness of the world, and our temperament or personality," we will have some idea of who we are and what we have been called to do. But we are also reminded that the "discovery of vocation happens in community." Do you belong to any community that is close enough to give you honest feedback on these four indicators of vocation? How can this group contribute to that process?

4. Be True to Yourself

"The essential and mature act is simple: come to a full realization of who you are and what you have been gifted to do, and embrace it eagerly" (pp. 49–53). In other words, do who you are.

   a. To what degree are you living out your vocation at this time of your life?

What barriers are preventing you from doing so, if any? How can they be overcome?

   b. It is noted in *Courage and Calling,* Smith writing, that as a husband, one of his priorities is "to enable my wife to discover, embrace and fulfill her vocation, a vocation that will certainly be a complement to mine but which will have an internal and inherent integrity and focus of its own."

Comment. If you agree with Smith's statement, how will it impact your criteria for a life partner (if you are married or are considering marriage)?

5. The Need Does Not Determine the Call (pp. 53–55).

Do you agree? If you do, what is there to prevent you from becoming calloused and insensitive to the many needs in your communities that may not correspond to your calling? Consider this: how have you let "need" derail you in the past from what was most important and closest to what

God was calling you to do?

Interacting with Scripture

Re-read Romans 12:3–8.

1. What does Paul expect of the Christians in Rome? (v. 3)

2. What is the basis for what you should be doing in the body of Christ? (v. 6–8)

3. Do you have some idea as to what are your capacities and strengths?

4. Are your choices concerning vocation and ministry congruent with your strengths?

For Further Reading

Brennfleck, Kevin and Kay Marie Brennfleck. "Mapping Your Design." Chap. 3 in *Live Your Calling: A Practical Guide to Finding and Fulfilling Your Mission in Life.* San Francisco, CA: Jossey-Bass, 2005.

Supplementary Questions to Help in Journaling

1. List down your primary strengths and abilities.

2. List down the things you enjoy doing.

3. What are your primary burdens? What keeps you awake at night?

4. As you reflect over your abilities, joys, and burdens, what clues do you get as to your calling?

3

CHAPTERS IN OUR LIVES

Focus: Following Our Vocation in the Different Chapters of Our Lives

Scripture for Meditation
Luke 2:41–52

Study Questions

1. *Courage and Calling* reminds us that ". . . the same vocational questions actually follow us through the whole course of our lives: Who am I, and who has God called me to be?" (pp. 57–70)

The observation is made that it is helpful to think of adult life in terms of three distinct phases:

- From adolescence into Early Adulthood, which happens around twenty years of age.
- From Early to Mid-Adulthood, a stage that begins in the mid-thirties and can last until our mid-fifties.
- From Mid-Adulthood to the Senior Years, something that begins around sixty years of age.

These are very rough approximates of the time when we will move through these chapters in our lives. On the whole, where do you find yourself, at least in terms of biological age?

2. The observation is made that the most critical transition is the move from adolescence into adulthood (pp. 58–62). Indeed, "vocational integrity and vitality are only possible if there is a break—a break from parents, from home, from adolescence." As we break from parents we move into "full adulthood' where God really becomes our Father, our parent.

Family systems theory calls this transition "differentiation," a stage of life where we are "not shaped unduly by the criticism or praise of others, so that we are able to live by our own convictions and by our own conscience . . . ."

   a. Take a long hard look at yourself. Irrespective of your biological age, to what degree have you successfully made this transition?

   b. To what degree do you know who you are and not just who your parents and others say you are?

   c. To what degree are you choosing to do what you believe God wants you to do and not what your parents or others want you to do?

   d. What needs to happen in your life right now to help you in this foundational transition if you are still largely stuck in adolescence?

3. Then consider that the Early to Mid-Adulthood stage of life is when "we move directly and intentionally into our vocation, understanding what our vocation is and accepting, indeed embracing, the call of God" (pp. 62–68).

That is because it is only in our mid-thirties that we begin to really know ourselves. ". . . Clarity for vocational purposes can only come after we have lived with ourselves long enough . . . ." Only then are we ready to face some critical questions

a. If we are gifted in more than one area, "we need to discern and affirm what is most significant to us and what brings the fullest expression of our identity." "We cannot be all things to all people. We need to choose, and our choices will mean saying no to some alternatives and eagerly embracing others."

To do this we need to do two things:

We must "accept with grace our limitations and move as quickly as we can beyond illusion about who we are."

"Second, it means that we accept the responsibility that comes with our gifts and abilities, and acknowledge with grace what we can do."

To what degree have you said no to what you are not, in order to say yes to who you are?

Has it been difficult or easy? What were some of your major difficulties in making this critical choice?

b. Note then the results of making this critical decision:

- Courage to do what is right even if it entails suffering and/or going against the status quo.
- Commitment and guidance to a path of life-long learning.
- The capacity to bounce back from failure and setbacks.
- The ability to embrace a healthy routine of

rest and Sabbath renewal.

To what degree have you experienced any of the above results of knowing and embracing your vocation?

  c. "Only as we accept ourselves and become completely ourselves—without pretense, envy or illusion—are we able to give ourselves fully to God and to others in generous service."

How much emphasis is there on "knowing yourself" in your church? Your fellowship? Your company? Your family?

If vocational self-knowledge is so important, why doesn't it receive more attention than it does?

What are some practical steps you can take right now if you are still unsure of your vocational identity?

4. "As Christians we may retire from our job or career, but we do not lose our vocation" (pp. 68–74).

We need to acknowledge that there are changes that come with our senior years, namely physical limitations, and the loss of "formal structures of power and influence." Indeed, consider that "when we are over sixty years of age we might be only beginning to discover our vocation or to fulfill it in a meaningful way."

  a. If you are already retired from your job or career, what are some key changes you have experienced in terms of the pursuit of your vocational calling?

If you are not yet retired, how do you feel as you think about retirement?

How do you plan to pursue your vocation in your senior years?

  b. An important point: Whatever our vocation, it

should be characterized by wisdom and blessing in our senior years.

Wisdom is the contribution of "words of counsel, admonition and encouragement." Blessing is "simply to affirm—to take particular delight and joy in someone in a manner that is neither judgmental nor prescriptive."

If you are in your senior years, do you find yourself committed to a life of providing wisdom for, and blessing others? Do you find your contribution welcomed? Why, or why not?

c. You do not need to be a senior to share wisdom with others and to bless others. Is your life committed to affirming others regardless of whatever stage of life you are in?

If you are not yet a senior, do you have seniors in your life who bless you and help provide wisdom for the critical issues of your life?

d. In retirement we let go of traditional and formal symbols of power, the roles and offices we held when we had a career. Our ability to make a difference then "is rooted in the quality of our lives and in our ability to give wisdom and blessing rather than in any particular role or responsibility we might have."

What does this tell us about the need to nurture our life in Christ at whatever stage of life we are in? How do you nurture your life in Christ at this juncture of your life?

Finally, note that vocation is dynamic in character. For most of us, a sense of call will come at three different times in our life: before or during the transition to adulthood, during midlife, and when we make our transition into our senior years.

The primary question we need to answer at all times, however, is this:

"What is God calling me to do here, in this place and at this time, so that I can be a conduit of life and grace to others?"

When was the last time you asked yourself this question? What was your answer? If you were to ask this question now, what would your answer be?

Interacting with Scripture

Read Luke 2:41–52.

1. When is it appropriate to be under the care and authority of our earthly parents? (v. 51). When is it time to embrace who we are in the eyes of our Heavenly Father irrespective of the expectations of our earthly parents? (v. 49)

2. Have you undergone this "individuation" process? If not, do you need to?

3. Identify the areas of growth mentioned in v. 52's summary of Jesus's maturation. What does it mean to be mature in those areas at your present age?

For Further Reading

Brennfleck, Kevin and Kay Marie Brennfleck. "Planning Your Journey." Chap. 9 in *Live Your Calling: A Practical Guide to Finding and Fulfilling Your Mission in Life.* San Francisco, CA: Jossey-Bass, 2005.

Supplementary Questions to Help in Journaling

1. For young adults: What did your parents want you to be when you grew up? How does this correspond with what you are feeling called to?

2. For mid-age adults: What are your strengths; but just as important, what are your limitations—so that in accepting what we are able and gifted to do, we can devote ourselves and give focus to what it is that we are being called to be and do?

3. For senior adults: What deep desire or longing can now be expressed in your life; a desire only possible as you "let go" of the structures of mid-life? And where do you need to "let go" of positions of power and control?

4

As Unto the Lord: The Pursuit of Excellence, Truth, Diligence and Generosity

Focus: Fundamental Virtues We Should Bring to Our Work

Scripture for Meditation
2 Timothy 2:14–21*

Study Questions

We are reminded that we all long for work that is "meaningful and significant, work that brings us joy." There are at least four qualities of vocational integrity identified in Paul's letters to Timothy—excellence, truth, diligence and generosity (pp. 83–85).

1. Excellence: ". . . we are given gifts and capacities and that to be true to ourselves we must exercise them to the best of our ability" (pp. 85–87).

---

* Consider reading all of 2 Timothy, with a notebook in which you identify all the ways in which character matters.

a. Do you find yourself intentionally seeking to do your best at work? Why, or why not? What motivates you to do your best work?

b. Note this comment in *Courage and Calling*: "In the end, only you and God know if you did your best." What tends to discourage you and inclines you to accept mediocrity when you do?

c. What are some practical ways to measure "our best?" In what ways can we prevent ourselves from falling into either mediocrity or "workaholism" or perfectionism?

2. Truth: "Good and rewarding work, work that is done 'unto the Lord,' is offered in the service of truth; it is truthful—full of truth" (pp. 87–89).

a. We note that "integrity requires a fundamental honesty—with our customers or clients, our employees and our stockholders."

How difficult is it to be consistently honest in your particular job situation? What are the particular pressure points—from your employer or supervisor, from clients, or from government or civil authorities?

b. We also note that a commitment to truth and truthfulness must be complemented with "a gracious, teachable spirit." Indeed a true commitment to truth must be based on a spirit of teachability.

Are you a teachable person? How do you feel when someone seeks to correct you? Do you find yourself becoming more or less teachable as you grow older?

c. A commitment to truth also means that we keep our word. This includes the commitment "to live our lives in a manner that is consistent with (our) professed values." As Christians we profess a commitment to ethical values that we hold to be from God, like the Ten Commandments.

If we were to poll those closest to you, e.g., your colleagues, your closest friends, your family, etc., do you think they will say that you are trying to live out what you profess to be true and right?

3. Diligence: "Diligence involves doing our work with a care and commitment that does not waver depending on the level of affirmation we are getting on a particular day. We do what we do because it needs to be done" (pp. 89–90).

   a. "I am increasingly convinced that there is no task that is easy in itself." Therefore "we must watch out for the patterns of 'corner cutting'."

On a scale of 1–10 how you would you rate your daily work in terms of its difficulty? How do you motivate yourself to give your all on days when the work really gets to you? Do you ever "cut corners"? Is it right to say that this cannot be reconciled with a Christian work ethic?

   b. Note the warning: We should not confuse "diligence and hard work with hectic activity or overwork." We need to be on guard against the crippling effects of perfectionism. Do you see yourself prone to overwork and perfectionism? How can you draw a line between diligence and overwork— what is the dividing line for you and how can you recognize when this line has been crossed?

4. Generosity: ". . . see every human being as having incomparable worth and significance" and therefore deserving of

"generous service" (pp. 90–92).

  a. Note that we need to distinguish generous service from calculated service. One is given freely while the other "counts the costs and considers the return . . . ." Though we may be paid for our work, we do our work as unto the Lord.

How can we attend to matters of a fair wage and just payment for our work, but also sustain a vision and passion for generous work and service?

  b. Generous service enables those we serve "to grow, mature, stand alone, and eventually give, as we serve one another in interdependence." False service, on the other hand, creates dependence.

Reflect on what this means for you at this point in your life and work. What are the practical indicators that through your work you are empowering others rather than creating unwarranted or inappropriate dependency?

(Examples: The English language teacher's passion is to free the student to speak English and no longer need the instructor; the person who sells cars is eager to see someone purchase a vehicle that will serve them well for many years; the family counselor delights that the couple with a marriage crisis have matured and are able to resolve conflicts on their own without the counselor's intervention.)

  c. There is a warning against sacrificing "fundamental relationships—such as with spouse and children" in a "misguided generosity." What are your "fundamental relationships" at this point in your life? What practical steps can one take to ensure that these are sustained?

5. Sabbath: It is noted that for the Hebrews, the weekly Sab-

bath was a time of rest but it was also a reminder that "their ultimate identity was not wrapped up in their work; they belonged to God" (pp. 92–94).

a. Do you have a sabbath day worked into your weekly schedule? If that day is a Sunday, how restful is it? If Sunday is a necessary work day for you, what other day could or does serve as your sabbath day?

b. Our sabbath day is not just a day off. We are called to sabbath rest as we are called to work. Both sabbath rest and work are valid in their own rights. Does your church take sabbath rest seriously? How much encouragement do you get from your church to ensure that you experience sabbath rest?

How about you? Do you take sabbath rest as seriously as your work? Why or why not?

Interacting with Scripture

Read Colossians 3:22–4:1.

(Paul is talking to slaves and masters but there are principles here that can inform our attitude towards our work as Christians.)

1. How are Christians to do their work according to Paul? How are you to do your work if you are in a position of leadership and management?

2. What are the incentives that Paul gives for one to work like that?

3. Reflect on your own attitudes toward your daily work. Do they incorporate the attitudes Paul is calling for? Why or why not?

For Further Reading

Ford, David F. "Power, Virtue, and Wisdom: The Shaping of Character." Chap. 3 in *The Shape of Living: Spiritual Directions for Everyday Life.* Grand Rapids, MI: Baker Books, 1997.

Supplementary Questions to Help in Journaling

1. Do you give your best at work? Why or why not?

2. What are the things that should characterize a Christian worker?

3. The Bible prescribes a schedule of six days of work and one day of sabbath rest. To what degree does your life follow this rhythm?

4. What would an ideal sabbath day look like for you? What would be its ideal features or elements? What do you need to do to ensure that your sabbath has these features most of the time?

5. There will always be external factors and pressures that will affect your ability to find sabbath. Instead of focusing on them, consider what you can do to strengthen the place of sabbath in your life.

5

Thinking Vocationally

Focus: The Advantages of Living Vocationally

Scripture for meditation
Matthew 25:14–30

Study Questions

1. Note that there are a number of advantages if we were to think vocationally, all variations "on the theme of freedom from the burden of pretense, freedom to be who we are truly called to be" (pp. 96–99).

    - We are freed from comparing ourselves to one another.
    - We are freed from artificial standards of excellence.
    - We are freed from the burden of trying to please everyone.
    - We are freed from urgency and the tyranny of time.
    - We are freed to love others.

    a. Of these five expressions of freedom, which are

most pertinent to the present stage of your life?

b. What practical steps can you take to experience more freedom?

c. What can your church community do to help her members experience more of the freedoms that come from living vocationally?

2. Note also a number of obstacles to living vocationally (pp. 99–107).

- A sacred-secular distinction in the understanding of vocation—the failure to "appreciate the sacredness of all vocations."
- Failure to distinguish between vocation and career or occupation—thereby tying our sense of vocation "to a particular place or role."
- The three classic temptations—in our work, we are sidetracked by the "desire for power, the desire for material security and comfort, and the desire for fame or prestige."
- Misguided sense of duty—either from a sense of obligation to justify one's chosen formal education, or, in blind compliance to authority figures.
- Failure to appreciate our limits—we either overstate the limitations in our lives, or we function as though we have no limits at all.

a. Take a long hard look at this list of obstacles to living vocationally. Do you recognize any of them as having had a significant impact on your life as you have sought to discern and follow your vocation?

b. Which obstacles are you currently struggling with?

c. How do you think you can respond to them?

Any suggestions from the group?

3. In order to think vocationally, it is suggested that we need two "essential capabilities" (pp. 107–111).

First, we need the capacity for retrospection. As we reflect on our lives, we will be able to "see and appreciate our own stories and the footprints of the Spirit through the course of our lives." Critical self-knowledge comes from knowing our "personal history." Indeed, we are reminded that "it is in the telling of our story that we come to clarity about what is important to us and about what, more than anything else, we know we are called to do."

a. Do you take time for retrospection? What have you learned about yourself from this form of reflection?

b. If you do not tend to be retrospective, is it merely a matter of finding the time, or are there other factors that keep you from this practice?

Next, we note the need and the ability to be "fully present." Indeed we are warned about an unhealthy form of retrospection that keeps us "living in the past." Instead, "we look back so that we can be fully present to the current situation, to the current moment, to the real circumstances of our current life mission." In this regard, it is important to remember that often "God leads us a step at a time."

c. Are you focused? If not, what is it that tends to distract you or keep you from effective vocational focus at this point in your life?

4. Finally, remember that "to think and act vocationally we must think and act intentionally" (p. 111). And this means that we are not merely acted upon; we do not merely react to our circumstances and to what is forced on us. Rather, we respond thoughtfully, and our actions are focused and purposeful.

   a. To what degree are you living the life that you believe God wants you to live? Or is your life but a reaction to people and circumstances?

   b. Are you confident enough about your vocational calling to be able to say either "yes" or "no," as required, to the many demands of life?

Interacting with Scripture

Read Matthew 25:14–30.

1. Who decided what amount of talents was to be given to the various servants? Should we then compare our vocations with those of others? Why are we tempted to do so?

2. Instead of comparing our vocation with the vocations of others, what should we be focusing on?

3. How can you be a good steward of your life, especially of your strengths and abilities?

For Further Reading

Brennfleck, Kevin and Kay Marie Brennfleck. "Called to be You." Chap. 2 in *Live Your Calling: A Practical Guide to Finding and Fulfilling Your Mission in Life*. San Francisco, CA: Jossey-Bass, 2005.

Supplementary Questions to Help in Journaling

1. Are you at peace with who you are and who God made you to be? Are you able to find the freedom that comes with not wishing you were someone else? How did that happen?

2. What difference would it make in your life if you spent less time wishing you were someone else?

6

Courage and Character

Focus: Finding the Courage to Follow Our Vocation

Scripture for meditation
2 Timothy 1:6–7; Joshua 1:1–9

Study Questions

1. "God has not given us a spirit of fear, but of power and of love and of a sound mind" (2 Timothy 1:7 NRSV). Note then the significance of this: "If we embrace our vocation and thrive within that to which God has called us, it will first and foremost be because we are women and men of courage." Read through the examples of courage that are provided on pages 115–117.

   a. How do you feel as you read about these people of courage? What impressed you?

   b. What would it look like for you to be a person of courage in your circumstances?

2. But then, of course, we need to note that true courage has certain qualifiers: "wisdom, moral integrity, gratitude,

humility and patience" (pp. 117–121).

Wisdom. ". . . True courage must be marked by prudence." Men and women of authentic courage are individuals who do what needs to be done rather than being taken by big schemes or mere drama. They were people who were marked by their "determination to do what needed to be done and to say what needed to be said in the routine of every day."

a. In your circumstances, how might wisdom and prudence help you to respond with courage?

b. Where can you go for wisdom for your circumstances—a good book, a mentor advisor, perhaps?

Moral Integrity. "Our private lives and our work in the world are part of a whole." Therefore true courage must go hand in hand with moral integrity, for example, in the areas of financial honesty and sexual integrity.

c. What steps can you take to move towards greater moral integrity in your life? What areas would need special care?

d. What safeguards or practices should be part of your life to sustain a greater level of integrity?

Gratitude and Humility. "Without these virtues, moral integrity is nothing more than moralism and judgmentalism." We note further that gratitude and humility are characterized by things like grace, forgiveness, compassion, a sense of humor, and a teachable spirit. Indeed, we note that "humility frees us to celebrate the gifts and abilities of others rather than to feel diminished by them."

e. Would your colleagues think of you as a grateful person? Or would they experience you more as a person who regularly complains about life, work, others and your circumstances?

f. Do your colleagues and co-workers experience you as someone who celebrates the strengths and achievements of others without jealousy or envy? Why?

Patience. "True courage is characterized by patience—patience with God, whose work is often imperceptible and slow, patience and generosity of spirit with others, and patience with ourselves."

i. Do your colleagues experience you as a patient person? With whom are you most impatient—God, others, or yourself?

j. How can you further cultivate the fruit of patience in your life?

3. We are challenged to have the courage to "be who we are and to do what we are called to do . . . ." Samuel Johnson, for example, was a man who "refused to be a victim and to blame his circumstances and his limitations on anyone" and who saw envy as "a waste of energy" (pp. 121–122).

a. Do you find it difficult to accept the skills and abilities that God has given you?

b. What can you do so that you are more inclined to embrace who you are, and resolve to be the best you that you can be?

4. The courage to be who we are also requires that we are honest about our fears. "Acknowledging our fears does not in itself make us courageous or justify our actions. But it is a start. When we acknowledge our fears, we can ask if

they are legitimate; we can ask if we are really living in faith, hope and love, or whether our fears are nothing but rationalizations for actions that are less than noble" because "only with courage will we have the capacity to move beyond convention, compliance and imitation and truly be who we are called to be" (pp. 122-124).

  a. What are the primary fears that hold you back from embracing your vocation? Failure? Loss of financial security? Loss of status? Disapproval of key people in your life? Fear that others will not understand? Other?

  b. What are some realistic ways to confront and overcome your fears? Do you want to?

5. We need to acknowledge that living vocationally will not be easy. We will need help. Specifically, we need two things. One, we need the grace of God, the confidence that "God goes with us and fills us with his spirit." Next, we need the encouragement of others. When we encourage one another "we grant to one another that quality, that virtue, that intangible inner strength that enables us to rise above the fears that so easily cripple us."

  a. What can you do to appropriate the grace of God? What are some specific ways by which you can receive the grace that God wants to give you?

  b. How can others be an encouragement to you? Have you allowed yourself to be encouraged? How can you be an encouragement to others?

Interacting with Scripture

Read Joshua 1:1–9.

1. What impresses you in reading these verses—especially with regard to the task to which Joshua is called?

2. Notice how many times God tells Joshua to be strong and courageous. Why did God do that? As you read, what impresses you with regard to your own circumstances?

3. Thinking back, were there times in your life when you knew what was the right thing to do but struggled to find the courage to do it? At times like these, how do we find the courage to do the right thing?

For Further Reading

Brennfleck, Kevin and Kay Marie Brennfleck. "Conquering the 'Calling Blockers'" and "Fear." Chap. 11 and Chap. 12, respectively, in *Live Your Calling: A Practical Guide to Finding and Fulfilling Your Mission in Life.* San Francisco, CA: Jossey-Bass, 2005.

Supplementary Questions to Help in Journaling

1. Do you tend to be more "timid" or more "courageous"? If timid, what might you do to foster greater intentionality and courage? If courageous, what might you do to foster a courage that is marked by wisdom and prudence?

2. Where have you found the courage to do what you needed to do? Think about specific examples in your life when you had to do things you were afraid of because it was the right thing to do.

3. How does one nurture a spirit of integrity so that we live by the values we espouse? How do you do it?

7

The Capacity to Learn

Focus: Learning How to do Life-long Learning

Scripture for meditation
Proverbs 2:1–5; 4:5–7

Study Questions

"Our potential for vocational growth and long-term vocational vitality exists in direct proportion to our capacity to learn." Indeed, "Knowing how to learn is critical to our capacity to respond and adapt to change" (pp. 127–130).

1. Pivotal to our vocations is our ability to be continuous learners, in both our work and in our relationships. "Work is task-oriented, with a focus on achievement. Relationships are people-oriented, with a focus on feelings. The challenge of true personal maturity is to develop the capacity to be complete and effective in both areas."

   a. Are you intentionally and proactively seeking to live a life of life-long learning? If yes, how are you putting this commitment into practice?

b. The categories of work and relationships go together; strength in one strengthens our capacity in the other. How would this be the case in your life circumstances?

c. Identify one point where learning is called for—in your relationships, and then also in your work. If you are a new parent, then you have the challenge of learning how to raise a child; and if you have a job change or a change in your work circumstances, then learning will be called for.

2. It is helpful to think of four primary ways in which people learn (pp. 130–135).

- Cognitively—through lectures and reading.
- Socially—through small-group discussions where conversation is the key to learning.
- By doing—learning through the actual experience of doing something.
- Through observation—to stand outside the event, watching from a safe distance, before actively engaging.

a. What is your preferred way of learning? How can you further exploit this preference to grow in the things you need to learn?

b. But we also we need to learn to learn in all four approaches. Which of the other three approaches do you need to work on next? Why? For example: if your circumstances require that you learn something that can only be learned by "doing" (such as driving a car), then you need to learn by doing, even if this is not your preferred mode.

3. Let's remember that whatever approach we use, we will still need to be patient as all learning takes time. We also need to keep track of our progress through evaluation and review. "If we are going to master anything . . . we need to learn through the observations and critique of others" (pp. 135–138).

   a. How do you feel when you have to be evaluated by others? Why? If you feel threatened by the evaluations of others, how can you work towards a time when you can be appropriately positive about being evaluated?

   b. We also note the critical role that mentors play in our learning processes. Good mentoring is "the capacity to bring hope and encouragement, believing in people so that they can learn, grow and embrace all that they are called to be."

Do you have such people in your life? If you have, can you select one or two and explain how they do their mentoring and how that has impacted you? If you have no mentors in your life, how can you go about seeking some people to be your mentors? Are you actively mentoring others?

4. Finally, we need to affirm that learning without wisdom is incomplete because wisdom is something that "integrates our learning, giving focus to it and ultimately enabling us to mature as individuals through it." Note Proverbs 4:5–7 as one of many biblical passages that call for the acquisition of wisdom (pp. 139–141).

Wisdom is "the capacity to respond to the developments around us with strength, to have the skills to embrace change and new challenges with ingenuity and to become mature emotionally through difficult setbacks and disappointments."

a. Is wisdom, as the goal of life and learning, emphasized within the Christian community of which you are a part? How does your community define wisdom?

b. There are a number of ways that we can grow in wisdom. One of these is that we understand and apply the knowledge that we have—that we act on what we are learning. Is there something you know or understand that needs to be put into practice?

c. Another is retrospection, making "life itself the curriculum" from which we learn. What can you do so that you draw more wisdom from your life? What practices or exercises can you use to be more intentional in this regard?

d. Journal writing is also a helpful discipline. Do you maintain a journal and write in it regularly? If yes, share how you go about keeping your journal. If no, share how you might begin to maintain one.

Interacting with Scripture

Read Proverbs 2:1–15.

1. What importance is placed on the acquisition of wisdom and understanding?

2. What are the results of acquiring wisdom and understanding?

3. Nowadays we are called to life-long learning. What are you learning in your life right now? How are you pursuing this learning?

4. How does one embark on a journey of growing in wisdom?

For Further Reading

Everist, Norma Cook. "Lifelong Learning in the Faith Community." Chap. 4 in *The Church As Learning Community*. Nashville, TN: Abingdon Press, 2002.

Supplementary Questions to Help in Journaling

1. Think of someone in your life that you consider wise. What qualifies this person as a wise person? What are the qualities that you value in this person?

2. In today's "information age," we are encouraged to a life of life-long learning. What books are you currently reading? If you are not a "reader" how do you prefer to learn the things you need to learn?

3. What are some key areas in which you want to do more study in the next five years? Why these areas? How will you go about doing it?

8

The Cross We Bear: Difficulty and Emotional Maturity

Focus: How to be Emotionally Healthy

Scripture for meditation
2 Corinthians 4:7–18

Study Questions

We are reminded that "No one is immune from pain; it is a part of the package that comes with life." Therefore we should not be taken by surprise when we encounter difficulty in life; and we need to consider the implications of this reality when it comes to career, work and vocation (pp. 143–144).

1. Where and how has pain and difficulty intersected your life? Depending on how comfortable you are to do so, share about one such experience, particularly as it relates to your work and career.

2. Because pain and suffering are part of life and work, we

need to make sense of our difficulties, "to see what significance it has for our capacity to fulfill a vocation." Indeed "there is hardly anything more critical to personal and vocational development than the nature of our response to difficulty, setbacks, rejection, disappointment or suffering."

And so, some working principles are needed to guide us through the difficult stretches of our lives (pp. 144–148).

- We can trust God and grow in our trust of God, because we know that God is bigger that all wrong and evil and that God is with us through it all;
- Our experience of difficulty enables us to grow in faith, hope and love; difficulty is the real test of our emotional and vocational maturity;
- Difficulty is part of the way in which the cross intersects our lives, and it is thus part of how God works through us for the sake of others.

Therefore we need to be alert to a "victim mentality" in the face of our difficulties. We have a choice as to how we respond to the difficulties in our life. We can allow the difficulty and suffering we go through to become "the means of grace to ourselves and to others."

a. What lessons have you learned through times of difficulty in your life?

b. We cannot choose whether or not we encounter difficulties in our lives. But we can choose how we respond to them. Take an honest look at how you feel about the pain and setbacks of your life. Have you responded as a victim? Have you reached a place in your life where you can process your difficulties in a positive way?

3. Consider what we need to do if we are to respond positively to pain and tragedy (pp. 148–156).

- We need to forgive those who have wronged us, beginning with our parents.
- We need to identify and accept the limitations and losses in our lives.
- We need to accept whatever pain that is inherent in our vocation.
- We need to be able to respond positively to whatever failure and setbacks we encounter in life.
- We need to see that it is our ability to accept suffering in what we do that enables us to differentiate vocation from careerism.

a. How would describe your relationship with your parents (whether or not they are still living)? What are things for which you can thank God for them? What are some areas where you may need to forgive them?

b. Jesus makes it clear that his followers are to forgive those who have wronged them (Matthew 6:12, 14–15). It is hard to forgive those who have wronged us badly. In the past, what challenges have you had to face in order to forgive? And is there now a situation that calls for you to practice forgiveness—some unresolved wrong that may keep you from embracing your future?

c. "Whatever the limitations we face, we will not live

with joy unless we learn to accept our losses with grace and choose to live in peace within the limits of our lives."

Have you learned to do this? How does one know whether a limitation is meant to be accepted or meant to be overcome?

d. "When we follow Jesus, we follow him to the cross; we bear a cross. Consequently, it is reasonable to conclude that in some form a cross will mark every vocation; there will be some way in which the pain of a broken world intersects with our call."

Have you been with your vocation long enough to identify some of the painful areas that come with it? Have you come to terms with them? Learned from them?

e. There are some failures that just have to be accepted. If the failures were due to our mistakes we can learn from them and then move on. We must not exaggerate the significance of our failures or get paralyzed by self pity. Otherwise we might get crushed by our failures "when we should probably merely close that door of our life, cut our losses and move ahead."

Do you find yourself prone to self-pity? If yes, how can you move beyond that? How does one close the door and move on after a major failure? What if other people make it hard for you to move on after a failure?

4. Consider that "emotional development may be the factor that more than any other determines whether we will become all we are called to be." And so it is essential that we take emotional health seriously—indeed, that we actu-

ally pursue emotional maturity. Here are six signs of emotional health (pp. 156–160).

- You know your feelings and are able to draw on them in making significant decisions rather than having your decisions sabotaged by your emotions.
- You are able to persist in the face of setbacks and disappointment.
- You are able to recognize the feelings of others and, as appropriate, empathize with them.
- You are able to express your emotions honestly in appropriate settings.
- You do not use emotional blackmail to get your way.
- You are able to respond to both praise and criticism with grace.

a. To what extent would you say that these qualities mark you?

b. Where do you see a need for more growth and personal development and how can you begin to attend to this area of your life and relationships?

5. There are a number of ways that can help us grow in our emotional health. First we must begin by accepting the fact that we are emotional beings and by being brutally frank about the feelings we are going through. Only with such honesty can we begin any journey to emotional health. Next, "we can know emotional maturity and resilience when we learn to open our hearts to God and to one another" (pp. 160–162).

a. Are you someone who is in touch with your emotions? Are you someone who is able to accept whatever emotions you are going through, especially negative ones?

b. Do you find that your time of daily prayer is one in which you experience the grace and comfort of God? Do you have adequate private time with God?

c. Do you have key relationships in your life—friendships or a small group, perhaps—where you can reflect on what you are experiencing emotionally?

Interacting with Scripture

Read 2 Corinthians 12:1–12.

1. Paul talks about a person, probably himself, who has been given a very painful affliction. What catches your attention as you read these verses?

2. In response to this affliction, what was Paul's initial prayer?

3. What was God's response and what did Paul say he was learning through the affliction?

4. How can this give us a perspective for the painful struggles in our lives?

For Further Reading

Brennfleck, Kevin and Kay Marie Brennfleck. "Childhood Wounds." Chap. 16 in *Live Your Calling: A Practical Guide to Finding and Fulfilling Your Mission in Life*. San Francisco, CA: Jossey-Bass, 2005.

Supplementary Questions to Help in Journaling

1. Think back over your life. What was the most painful experience you have ever had? Why was it so painful?

2. Have you experienced significant healing from this experience? If no, how could you go about seeking healing? Do you want to be healed?

3. What are some lessons you learned from this painful experience?

9

Working With and Within Organizations

Focus: The Promise and Challenges of Working With Others

Scripture for meditation
1 Corinthians 12:12–31

Study Questions

1. It is a basic principle of life and work: "We fulfill our vocation in partnership with others. The most obvious form or expression of partnership is found in our relationship with the organizations in which we work and through which we invest our lives and our energies." Therefore "if we are going to be all that we are called to be, and to respond with skill, courage and grace to the call of God on our lives, we must develop the capacity to work with others in the context of organizational life" (pp. 163–165).

   a. Consider your work and vocation: who are those that you depend on—identifying not by name, but by capacity and role that they play? For example: a writer needs an editor and a publisher;

an artist needs a gallery; an athlete needs a trainer and coach.

b. Reflect on your present job. To what degree is your ability to carry out your work enhanced by working with others? Are you comfortable working with others?

2. To work well in organizations, we need to grow in certain qualities and capacities, including these three (pp. 165–166).

- We must be good listeners.
- We must be dependable.
- We have to respect others.

a. Read through the description of the three qualities (pp. 165–166). Then rate yourself on a scale of 1–5 for the three qualities.

b. Which of the three qualities needs the most work? Why do you think you are relatively weaker in that quality? What practical steps can you take right now to nurture that particular quality?

3. Next, consider that to be effective in organizations we need to do our own work well "in a way that takes account of the big picture" (pp. 167–170). In particular, we need to do our work in the context of three important aspects of the life of the organization, namely:

- The mission of the organization.
- The budget of the organization.
- Communications within the organization.

a. What is the mission of your organization? How

aware are others who work with you of the mission of your organization? Was the mission a factor when you chose to work with this organization? Why or why not?

b. Do you know what is the financial situation of your organization? Is it a for-profit or non-profit organization? How is the current cash flow situation of your organization? Do you agree with the values underlying how money is used in this organization? Are you in any way able to influence the way money is spent in your organization?

c. Are you satisfied with the level of communication in your organization? Do you have all the information you need to get your work done? Who needs to be informed of what you are doing to increase team effectiveness? What sorts of information do not need to be passed out and only add to unnecessary information overload?

4. A further requirement for working effectively within organizations is the need to think in terms of complementary capacities. Indeed the main reason we work within organizations is "because we need one another to achieve a common goal or purpose" (pp. 170–171).

a. What are your primary capacities and strengths? And where do you have need for the strengths and capacities of others?

b. How can you more intentionally enable others to thrive in their vocations—thinking specifically of your current work and occupation (in your office, or as part of your church community, etc.)?

5. Healthy organizations are places where power is shared. Traditionally, we note that in many organizations the power tends to flow from the top down (pp. 171–173). Therefore, we need to work at ways in which power can be shared, so that there is greater organizational effectiveness, such as:

- Empowering others.
- Adopting a win-win approach in negotiations.
- Learning together, including learning from others.
- Learning to converse well, with mutual respect.

a. Consider the sphere of your work and the organization of which you are a part. How is power exercised and how are decisions made?

b. Within the limitations of your role, how can you encourage a process that reflects shared power?

6. In all of this, we need to be reminded that we must learn to work "with and through the actual circumstances and potential of our situation rather than constantly fighting the limits and boundaries that we invariably face." It is a call to be rooted in what is, including working with the actual potential of an organization. It is learning to be grateful for the good things in an organization rather than always pining for some ideal situation that doesn't exist (pp. 173–175). Please note: it is very easy to complain and criticize; it is easy to see fault and note what is lacking in our workplaces. There is a time and place for critique; but at this point, consider what opportunities your workplace offers you to make a difference, within the limitations you have to work with.

a. What are the strengths of your organization? How might you be able to build on those strengths?

b. What opportunities does your organization give you for making a difference?

c. What do you need to watch for (in yourself) so that you can avoid feeling victimized by your workplace?

7. It is noted that to work well in organizations we must "learn to be effective in the midst of change" (pp. 175–176). To do that we need "a capacity to adapt to . . . changes and see them as opportunities for growth and learning."

a. How is your organization changing? How might you be able to learn and be creative in the midst of the change?

b. How do you feel about these changes? What encourages you? And what concerns you about the change that is coming?

8. Finally, consider this: "Most fundamentally, to thrive within organizations we must find congruence between ourselves and the organizations in which we serve" (pp. 176–184). That means people working in organizations "whose missions they own and whose values they can identify with."

That brings up the question of when it is appropriate to resign from an organization in which we are working. We note that our bias should be against job change as "the virtues of perseverance, patience, faithfulness and dedication are essential if we are going to fulfill our vocation."

There are a number of reasons that may justify our resigning from an organization:

- We have completed what we came to do.
- We are no longer effective.
- Our strengths are no longer needed in this place at this time.
- As a matter of conscience.

a. Do you find that by and large you find congruence between who you are and the organization in which you are presently working? If yes, what are the points of connection for you and if no, what are the indicators that you do not fit with this organization?

b. Note: our fundamental bias should be towards staying and not leaving. How many times have you changed organizations and/or jobs to date? Consider the last two job changes or moves: What were the reasons that made you decide to move? In retrospect, did you make a wise decision?

c. On the other hand, was there a time when you should have resigned but failed to do so? There are also reasons that make it hard for us to resign. We may be fearful of making a mistake. This is understandable but remember that "in most cases people who should resign stay much longer than they ought to."

Then there is the fear of financial insecurity. Though we must be aware of the need for proper financial management, let's beware of "unrealistic expectations about what financial security looks like" and placing our "lifestyle expectations ahead of vocational integrity." In your case, what might have been the reason for not resigning when you should have? What does this tell you about yourself?

Interacting with Scripture

Read 1 Corinthians 12:12–31.

1. What is one key reason we are put in churches where the members have different spiritual gifts? (v. 14–24)

2. What sort of spirit enables such a set-up to work? (v. 25–26)

3. To what degree can such principles be applied to non-Christian organizations?

For Further Reading

Brennfleck, Kevin and Kay Marie Brennfleck. "Going It Alone." Chap. 17 in *Live Your Calling: A Practical Guide to Finding and Fulfilling Your Mission in Life.* San Francisco, CA: Jossey-Bass, 2005.

Collins, Jim. *Good to Great: Why Some Companies Make the Leap and Others Don't.* New York: HarperCollins, 2001.

Supplementary Questions to Help in Journaling

1. Think through the last two or three job positions you had, and consider the following: what were the best working relationships I had, and which were the most stressful? Thinking about yourself, ask this: what did I do to make the good working relationships more effective, and what might I have done differently in making the stressful relationships less difficult?

2. In your current workplace: what are some of the immediate practices or perspectives you could bring to your daily work that could improve the quality of the working relationships you have? Remember: in the end, you cannot determine the behaviour and attitudes of another; but you can

take responsibility for your own capacity to work well with others.

3. If you are in an organization (or church) that is marked by significant conflict, how can you be a peace-maker in the mist of this difficult set of circumstances? What are you learning about yourself in this and what active steps can you take for the sake of the whole organization?

10

The Ordered Life: Between Solitude and Community

Focus: Basic Spiritual Disciplines to Help Us Finish Well

Scripture for meditation
Luke 6:12–19; Mark 1:35–42

Study Questions

1. *Courage and Calling* concludes with a chapter where we are reminded of the freedom that order brings if we are not to be "caught up in hectic, confused activity, or … left purposeless and confused about our identity and about what to do next." And so we can speak of an ordered life "in which both work and rest are embraced."

We note three guiding principles for an ordered life (pp. 185–190).

- Sustain clarity about what is important. "We must sustain a clear perspective of what really matters and what is truly important."
- Graciously accept the limitations of life.

"We cannot do all that we wish we could do, and we cannot be all things to all people. So we can stop trying to do everything."
- Create and embrace the spaces in your schedule. "Create margins in the day between activities; allow time for thinking, planning and conversation. . . . Begin the day with space for prayer and reflection."

Consider these three principles for an ordered life. How are you doing in each and what are the particular challenges for you in each of the three; consider sharing these insights with your group.

2. In order to live an ordered life, we need community (pp. 190–193). "We discern our vocation in community, and we fulfill it as we are anchored in mutual interdependence with others within community." Indeed it is within community that we encounter the presence of God.

This communion with others requires "conversation," the commitment to listen and to speak in our relationships with others.

a. Do you have three or four meaningful friendships? If not, are you able to identify why you have not been able to develop these essential relationships in your life?

b. Community life demands both listening and speaking. Take a moment to reflect on your conversational patterns. Do you do more listening or speaking? If you need to become a better listener what steps would you need to take? If you need to speak up more, how will you do it? How can your speech be more gracious and encouraging?

c. Are you in any accountability/spiritual friendship groups? If yes, share a little of your experience in your group. If no, would you consider taking some steps to join/form such a group?

3. Consider the example of Jesus as described in Mark 1:35–42. We see here that Jesus was a person who was both compassionate and lived with clarity of purpose, and significant here is that Jesus took time out for solitude, times when he could commune with His Father (pp. 193–196).

Note: "Solitude is essential for vocational clarity and integrity because it is in solitude that we are enabled to sustain a connection, a relationship, with the one who has called us." Journal writing is an exercise to help us keep track of our personal times with God.

a. What has been your experience with times of solitude? Do you have any? Do you look forward to them? What for you is the main obstacle to being alone with Jesus?

b. If indeed solitude is necessary to sustain a life of purpose and compassion how do you intend to incorporate this practice into your life?

c. Have you ever kept a journal? If yes, share how you did it and how you benefited from the exercise. If no, how could you begin to keep one?

4. And so *Courage and Calling* speaks of the "two poles—community and solitude—as the means by which we know the grace that enables us to live with faith, hope and love." They are essential in helping us to reach our ultimate goal, "to be women and men who know love and serve Jesus." But we also need to remember that some of our deepest long-

ings will not be fulfilled this side of heaven. "They await the reign of Christ." Hence we are free to do our best even in the midst of "disappointments, frustration and setbacks..." (pp. 196–197).

   a. What is the operative ultimate goal of your life? Is it to be a compassionate person serving Jesus? If so, how will this be evident in the quality of your daily life now? What difference does this make, when things are not going well for you? How can the fact of Jesus' coming again give us the strength to cope with the disappointments and unfulfilled potentials of this life?

   b. What are practical ways for you to experience both solitude and community as you move on in your life?

Interacting with Scripture

Read Luke 6:12–19.

1. Verses 17–19 record Jesus busy ministering and teaching. However there were two things he did before he ministered. What were they? See v. 12 and vv. 13–16.

2. How do you set apart time to be alone with God?

3. What is the quality of your life in community?

4. What are some basic disciplines you can put in place in your life to ensure adequate times of solitude with God and community with significant others?

For Further Reading

Nouwen, Henri J. M. *Making All Things New*. San Francisco, CA: Harper & Row Publishers, 1981.

Bonhoeffer, Dietrich. *Life Together*, trans. by Daniel W. Bloesch. Minneapolis, MN: Fortress Press, 1996.

Supplementary Questions to Help in Journaling

1. We are often exhorted to "finish well" in our lives. What does that mean to you, "to finish well?"

2. What are some factors that could sabotage any desire to finish well, but especially for you?

III

Final Exercises

Final Exercises

A. My personal mission in life—what I am called to do with the rest of my life.

1. Clues to my personal mission—looking at my history.

Draw up a simple timeline of your life. Draw a horizontal line with *Birth* at one end and *Now* at the other.

You may want to divide your timeline into some natural sections like:

1. Early childhood/Preschool
2. Primary school (Grades 1–6)
3. Secondary school (Grades 7–11/12,13)
4. Tertiary education
5. Early working life
6. Early working life to the present.

(Not all the sections will apply to everyone.)

For each of the sections, look for the times when the following occurred (this list is taken from Ben Campbell Johnson's book, *Hearing God's Call,* and reproduced with his kind permission):

1. The idea of a call came into your mind.
2. A person affirmed a gift God has given you.

3. A text from Scripture spoke to you about God's call.
4. You saw the pain of others and wondered what you could do to help.
5. Your own experience of pain drew you to others suffering the same kind of pain.
6. You felt very close to God.
7. You felt very restless in your work.
8. You noticed that your life was being shaped by a series of "gentle calls" from God.
9. Someone invited you to join an existing ministry.

Johnson's list is not an exhaustive one. You may also want to look at some of the burdens the Lord has laid on your heart, for example, to reach a particular people group for Christ, to start and run a business with Christian values, to help those afflicted by abject poverty, etc.

As you quietly reflect over your life, ask the Lord to bring to mind significant moments like the ones suggested in the list above. Believing that God is sovereign over your life, what does the presence of such "call" moments tell you about what the Lord wants you to do with your life?

2. Clues to my personal mission—looking at the abilities that God has given me.

We all have things that we do well. This could be a mix of natural talents, acquired skills and spiritual gifts. But they are all from God and are for His use.

Again Johnson gives some guidelines for a useful exercise.

He suggests that we draw up a grid with three columns. In the first column write down *the things you do well*. In the second column write down *the things you enjoy doing.* In the third calling write down *the things that others say you do well.*

After you have filled in the three columns prayerfully, take some time to meditate over what you have written. Look especially for items that appear in all three columns.

What conclusions can you draw as to some things that the Lord has enabled you to do well?

What does this tell you about your personal life mission?

3. Reflect on the above two exercises. Review your reflections from *Courage and Calling* Chapter Two and any further insights you gleaned from the group interaction.

Then write a short paragraph as to what you think the Lord wants you to do with the rest of your life.

Each of us is unique and God wants to do different things through different people. R. Paul Stevens gives us some contemporary examples of mission statements.

> Don Flow: "To create a car business that provides extraordinary service to its customers, develops its employees to their God-given potential and glorifies God in its culture, policies and systems."
>
> James M. Houston: "To break the alabaster jar of theological education in the world and not just for the church."

Remember to distinguish your calling from your paid job. Some of us are blessed by the fact that we are paid to do what we have been called to do. But some of us may have to pursue our vocation outside our paid employment.

B. Essential spiritual disciplines—what I need to do to help ensure that I remain faithful to my personal mission.

1. Personal spiritual disciplines.

What are some personal spiritual disciplines you will commit yourself to, to help ensure that you remain faithful to your personal life mission?

Examples: private prayer, Bible reading, reading of spiritual literature, journaling, periodic retreats, etc.

2. Communal spiritual disciplines.

What are some communal disciplines you will commit to, to help ensure that you remain faithful to your personal life mission?

Examples: accountability groups, receiving mentoring, seeking spiritual direction, etc.

3. Review your answers to the above two questions. Review also your responses to Chapter Ten of *Courage and Calling*. Write a short paragraph outlining your personal plan for spiritual growth based on the spiritual disciplines you have chosen. Be as detailed as you can.

C. Concluding action items.

1. Identify some key things that you have learned from this process (the reading of the book and the group discussion)—two or three things you have learned about yourself and about life.

2. Write down the two or three resolutions that have come out of this process; these are action items for the next twenty-one days. Note: it is most helpful to make the resolve a twenty-one-day commitment. After twenty-one days, it

will likely be part of the regular routine and rhythm of our lives.

3. What key new relationship do I need to seek—with a spiritual friend or mentor, with a pastor or church elder? Or perhaps with a counselor or family therapist? Or with a friend whom you meet with regularly to reflect on the subject of this book? Or with a small group that will meet regularly for support and encouragement?

4. Finally, write out your prayer of response to God—what you need to tell God as you come to the end of this process. Reflecting on your mission statement—who you are called of God to be and what you are called to do—what do you offer back to God by way of the response of your heart, both in terms of your prayer (what you are asking of God) and your commitment (what you are offering to God)? Be sure to share this with at least one other person.

Select Bibliography

Bonhoeffer, Dietrich. *Life Together*, trans. by Daniel W. Bloesch. Minneapolis, MN: Fortress Press, 1996.

Brennfleck, Kevin and Kay Marie Brennfleck. *Live Your Calling: A Practical Guide to Finding and Fulfilling Your Mission in Life*. San Francisco, CA: Jossey-Bass, 2005.

Everist, Norma Cook. *The Church As Learning Community: A Comprehensive Guide to Christian Education*. Nashville, TN: Abingdon Press, 2002.

Ford, David F. *The Shape of Living: Spiritual Directions for Everyday Life*. Grand Rapids, MI: Baker Books, 1997.

Johnson, Ben Campbell. *Hearing God's Call: Ways of Discernment for Laity and Clergy*. Grand Rapids, MI: William B. Eerdmans Publishing Company, 2002.

Mahan, Brian J. *Forgetting Ourselves on Purpose: Vocation and the Ethics of Ambition*. San Francisco, CA: Jossey-Bass, 2002.

Nouwen, Henri J. M. *Making All Things New*. San Francisco, CA: Harper & Row Publishers, 1981.

Schuurman, Douglas J. *Vocation: Discerning our Callings in Life*. Grand Rapids: William B. Eerdmans Publishing Company, 2004.

Smith, Gordon T. *The Voice of Jesus: Discernment, Prayer and the Witness of the Spirit.* Downers Grove, IL: InterVarsity Press, 2003.

Stevens, R. Paul. *Vocation, Work, and Ministry Resource Binder.* Vancouver, BC: Regent College, 1996.

Whyte, David. *Crossing the Unknown Sea: Work as a Pilgrimage of Identity.* New York: Riverhead Books, 2001.

Soo-Inn Tan grew up in Malaysia and is one of the founding directors of Graceworks Private Limited, a ministry committed to promoting spiritual friendship in church and society. He also serves as honorary associate pastor of Evangel Christian Church, Singapore. He has a BDS from the University of Singapore, a ThM from Regent College and a DMin from Fuller Theological Seminary. His primary passions include connecting the Word of God to the struggles of daily life, and the promotion of spiritual friendship. He is the author of *Making Sense: 52 Meditations for Heart and Mind*, and *Travel Mercies: Reflections from the Road Called Life*.

Gordon T. Smith grew up in Ecuador and is president of reSource Leadership International (formerly Overseas Council Canada), which works with other reSource affiliates to support and enable excellence in theological education in the developing world. Formerly Academic Dean and Associate Professor of Spiritual Theology at Regent College in Vancouver, British Columbia, he has also taught in the Philippines and at Canadian Bible College and Theological Seminary in Regina, Saskatchewan. He is the author of *Beginning Well*, *Courage and Calling*, *Listening to God in Times of Choice* and *The Voice of Jesus*.

www.ingramcontent.com/pod-product-compliance
Lightning Source LLC
Chambersburg PA
CBHW032020040426
42448CB00006B/685